LUCINDA'S AUTHENTIC JAMAICAN KITCHEN

LUCINDA'S AUTHENTIC JAMAICAN KITCHEN

LUCINDA SCALA QUINN · PHOTOGRAPHS BY QUENTIN BACON

LOCATION PHOTOGRAPHS BY KAREN MARSHALL

WILEY

JOHN WILEY & SONS, INC.

Copyright © 2006 by Lucinda Scala Quinn
Photography Copyright © 2006 by Quentin Bacon
Photography Copyright © 2006 Location photography by Karen Marshall

Published by John Wiley & Sons, Inc., Hoboken, New Jersey
Published simultaneously in Canada

Library of Congress Cataloging-in-Publication Data

Quinn, Lucinda Scala.
  Lucinda's authentic Jamaican kitchen / by Lucinda Scala Quinn ;
photographs by Quentin Bacon.— Rev. ed.
    p. cm.
  Includes index.
  ISBN 13-978-0-471-74935-6
  ISBN 10-0-471-74935-4 (cloth)
  1. Cookery, Jamaican. I. Title.
  TX716.J27Q57 2006
  641.597292—dc22
                        2005021371

Food Styling by Alison Attenborough
Prop Styling by Darienne Sutton
Design by Elizabeth Van Itallie

Printed in China.

10   9   8   7   6   5   4   3   2   1

FOR JENNY

CONTENTS

DESSERTS AND DRINKS   97

INTRODUCTION

Twenty years ago, I began writing this book. Ten years later, it was first published, and still now, it remains, for me, an ode to the country I love so much. As it has with so many visitors before me, Jamaica slowly crept into my soul over time by exposure to its beautiful land, people and culture. This book is a fan letter, a thank-you note, an invitation and an introduction

Over the years, many Jamaicans living away from their native land have thanked me for penning these recipes for the beloved dishes of their homeland—some having never learned to cook them—others having forgotten them as the contemporary fast and full culture of food has supplanted their family traditions. For this new, smaller, full-color version of the original collection, I've included the popular favorites.

Soursop juice, codfish fritters, fried plantain, stew chicken, pumpkin soup with dumplings, callaloo, ackee and salt fish, beef patties, roast yam and rum cake—these

A young man sorts through the "Irish;"—white potatoes being delivered from the countryside to the parish market.

Roadside herbalist holding wild plants for bush tea; a local folk remedy.

are tastes from the first few meals I enjoyed during a recent visit. The flavors from these classics are as vibrant as ever. Cooking styles and techniques are unchanged. The importance and value of shared meals remains prevalent. Dining is still heightened by the sensations that surround you: the wafting breeze, an intoxicating scent of flower blossoms and sounds of hummingbirds hovering and buzzing over dangling, radiantly colored bougainvillea plants.

British naturalist Philip Henry Gosse wrote almost two hundred years ago describing Jamaica's unique landscape. He sums up the sometimes intangible grip the island of Jamaica holds: "But the picture itself, the thousand things that cannot be enumerated, birds, insects, flowers, trees, the tone of the whole, the sunlight, the suffused sky, the balmy atmosphere, the variety of foliage, the massive light and shadow, the deep openings in the forest; all rich, new and strange." Gosse's observations portray a vivid picture, which is as redolent today as it was then.

Yet, modern life has evolved rather organically around the island. Newer, more direct roads connect major towns. American fast-food joints have inevitably cropped up, but the classic Jamaican beef patty—Jamaica's true indigenous fast food, the "hamburger" of Jamaica—still dominates. It has even developed to include more varieties and styles.

I'm constantly amazed that Jamaica, this little dot on the map of the world, is such a fecund environment not only for natural resources but also for original cultural exports like reggae music, which continues to inform music internationally.

The Jamaican cooking style springs from the many ethnic traditions that define Jamaica's culture today—Arawak Indian, Spanish, African, English, Creole, East Indian, Middle Eastern, Mexican and Chinese. The cuisine is an outgrowth of this eclectic population mix combined with Jamaica's bountiful local products, which thrive in its lush landscape.

The Spanish brought various fruits like plantain and citrus. The dish that today is known as escovitch fish comes from their escabèche or pickled fish preparation. As the Africans from many countries began to arrive as slaves, so did many of their indigenous dishes such as ackra and fufu. Fortunately, the geography was similar to West Africa, which enabled the production of familiar crops like yam and corn. Traces of English influence are everywhere—from pickled meats and salted fish to desserts called puddings that are more like cakes.

The culinary history gets more complex with the post-slavery influence from the new wave of indentured laborers from East India, China and the Middle East. Curries, sweet-and-sour preparations and Syrian dishes, such as kibbeh, exist in today's Jamaican cooking. Creole contributions like patties came during the days when troops were enlisted from the other West Indian islands for various war efforts.

The tenacious Jamaican Maroons, runaway slaves of the Spanish and British who fled into the island's rough mountainous interior and eventually won the right to self-government, originated the jerk tradition by hunting and preserving wild hogs with pimento, peppers and ash.

Jerking is a prime example of necessity creating tradition. To fully understand the evolution of Jamaican cuisine, one must also consider the difficult conditions under which much of the food was cooked and consumed. The majority African slave population had few protein resources and was forced to rely on plantation masters for moderate amounts of salted fish, which were blended with the staple vegetables. As cooks, they tended to the culinary needs of the Spanish and English table, which further contributed to today's hybrid preparations.

What survives is a national cuisine that stands on its own, yet it is often obscured under the label of Caribbean cooking. It isn't Cuban or Creole food; rather it is a unique style that has emerged from the island's personal history. Authentic Jamaican food, when it is cooked with understanding, nourishes the body, mind and soul.

So many foods and dishes are named from the rich language of the Jamaican people. All around the island are hand-painted signs that announce jerk centers, fish and bammy shacks, fruit vendors, groceries, etc., all with the most clever and inventive names, an invitation to any passing traveler.

Beckoning from any roadside are great, unsung cooks, too. In Annoto Bay in the Parish of St. Mary, there is one notorious seaside vendor who sells steamed fish and the

A marketplace vendor sits amongst her speciality; local leafy greens pak choy and calaloo.

rich golden broth known as fish tea at his self-named "human service station." Against the sound of rolling surf, a steady stream of local folks and travelers pull up by car or wander over on foot at lunchtime. An intoxicating scent, both sweet and saline, wafts from the gently simmering pots.

The infamous, indigenous Jamaican barbecue known as jerk thrives in the jerk mecca of Boston Beach in Portland. The road curves gently, leading out of town toward Boston Beach, where clouds of barbecue smoke billow from the jerk enclave. A spicy smell of burning pimento wood fills your nose. Strong, primitive wood structures house the jerk pits, each offering a variation on the same fare: jerk pork, chicken and sausage, roasted breadfruit and festival. This is a man's world. The meat is chopped, weighed and doused in spicy jerk sauce, eaten with sweet, crispy festival and washed down with cold Red Stripe beer. Reggae music pulsates in the background.

In the bustling capital city of Kingston is Hopeton's

Best Jerk Chicken at Northside Plaza. This popular, late-night jerk stop has been doing business in the same spot for twenty-five years. Three partners divide up seven nights during the hours of 4 p.m. and 4 a.m. Propped up on the curbside is a fifty-gallon drum, halved on a stand, that forms the grill with a cover. The smoke pours out of a makeshift chimney. Next to the grill a small table holds a round lignum vitae board for chopping the meat. Farther up the corner is a pushcart that sells the necessary drinks and cigarettes. Kingstonians from all walks of life stop in throughout the night, some taking the jerk to go, others standing around eating and chatting while a colorful group of characters hangs out nearby.

Roadside jelly coconut vendors sell this product to a constant stream of regular customers. For fresh coconut water known as Ital Coolaid, the top of a green coconut is expertly hacked off and served with a straw. Afterward, with a chip of the shell, you can eat the soft jelly inside for its concentrated nutritious goodness and sweet, sensuous texture.

Roasted yam and salt fish is featured at Melrose Hill on the road to Mandeville in Manchester, a famous roadside stop where cars pull over to be greeted by someone holding a piece of brown paper underneath a chopped, roasted yam and a small piece of grilled salt fish. It's eaten by taking a bite of roasted yam and nibbling off a tiny piece of the grilled, salted fish. The soft, smooth-textured yam is a perfect taste counterpoint to the chewy salt fish. The yams look like large logs sitting on top of the fire. Hanging from the rafters over the grill are fresh ears of corn, which are husked and toasted directly over the fires.

The south coast at Bluefields Bay in Westmoreland is well known for its roast turbot fish. Near the beach are roadside kiosks—a popular stop for overheated, road-weary truckers who travel the road connecting Kingston to Black River and Sav-La-Mar. The turbot fish has a dense, sweet-tasting flesh that is protected during cooking by its thick, leatherlike skin. Stuffed whole, it is laid over a metal griddle on a fire and periodically doused with a buttery liquid. Next to the grill stands a large soup pot filled with brewing fish tea. The soup combines pumpkin, chocho and green banana with the turbot for a thick, chowder-style consistency.

For a taste of the world-famous Blue Mountain coffee, visit the source by traveling up the narrow, winding roads that creep up into the Blue Mountains. Waterfalls spill out of mountain crevices. Tall trees with dense foliage form canopies over the glistening, rain-soaked bodies of local folks, who walk slowly with bunches of bananas balanced gracefully overhead. Sacks of coffee beans lie on the edge of the road. Men cut bamboo. A bright blue-painted hut on the hillside offers a cup of fresh Blue Mountain coffee. In the higher landscape, which is more lush and jungly, mist gently rises off the mountain tops only to be shadowed by a floating cloud. Tall, moss-covered trees boldly tower over the increasingly narrow road. Little pink wildflowers sprout from the banks of greenery. In the cool air, large fir trees thrive, juxtaposed against the long, perpendicular branches of bamboo. Long flaps of banana leaves bend overhead. From the peak, meadows appear as the view opens grandly onto the majestically sloping valleys.

Shrimp ladies sell bags of pepper shrimp in Middle Quarters in the Parish of St. Elizabeth, but for that story and more you've got to turn to the recipes and start cooking because "who feels it knows it," as the late Jamaican reggae artist Bob Marley sang. Anyone who has been to Jamaica and fallen in love with the local food will agree!

SNACKS,
SIDES
AND
SOUPS

COCONUT CHIPS

MAKES 2 CUPS

The sturdy texture of coconut makes it ideal for chips. People devour these snacks when served with cocktails. The coconut flavor really shines through when toasted.

1 coconut
1 teaspoon salt
2 teaspoons light or dark brown sugar
½ teaspoon ground white pepper

■ Preheat the oven to 350°F. Crack the coconut and drain the water. Remove the flesh from the hard shell. Peel off the brown skin from the flesh. Cut into thin strips.

■ Toss the coconut pieces with the salt, brown sugar and white pepper. Spread the coconut chips on a cookie sheet in one layer. Bake the chips until they are a deep golden color, about 10 minutes. Serve hot or cold.

BEEF PATTIES

MAKES 18 PATTIES (6 TO 9 SERVINGS; 2 PER PERSON FOR LUNCH)

The "hamburger" of Jamaica, a patty is the perfect snack or lunch. Layers of crispy dough enclose richly spiced meat. It is found on any corner in every town throughout the country. Prepared by few Jamaicans at home, patties are usually consumed on the run along with a box drink. Yet, they are simple and economical to prepare. Keep some uncooked in the freezer for a quick 15-minute bake-off. Also try the vegetarian version.

FOR THE PASTRY
2½ cups all-purpose flour
½ teaspoon salt
¼ teaspoon baking powder
2 tablespoons curry powder
½ cup butter (1 stick)
¾ cup ice-cold water

FOR THE FILLING
1 pound ground beef
1 onion, finely chopped
3 whole scallions, finely chopped
1 clove garlic, minced
2 Scotch bonnet peppers (any color), seeded and minced
1 teaspoon dried thyme or 2 sprigs fresh
¼ cup vegetable oil
2 teaspoons curry powder
1 teaspoon salt
½ teaspoon freshly ground black pepper
1½ to 2½ cups water
½ cup bread crumbs

FOR THE EGG WASH
1 egg, beaten with 1 teaspoon water

■ To make the pastry, combine the flour, salt, baking powder and curry powder in a large mixing bowl. Cut the butter into small pieces and add to the bowl. Working quickly and using your fingertips, squeeze together the flour mixture and butter and toss it together by scooping under the mixture with both hands. When the mixture resembles a very coarse meal, add the water to the bowl.

■ With floured hands, mix and squeeze the dough just until it forms a ball. Knead it once or twice to combine it fully (the less kneading, the better). Spread the dough into 2 pieces, flattening each into a thick pancake. Wrap in plastic and set them in the refrigerator to chill for at least 15 minutes. (The dough will keep in the refrigerator up to 5 days. Remove it from the refrigerator 30 minutes before using it.)

■ For the filling, mix together the beef, onion, scallions, garlic, peppers and thyme in a large bowl. In a large skillet, heat the oil over high heat until it is very hot, and add the beef mixture. Fry until the meat is brown and the moisture is evaporated, about 8 minutes. Add the curry powder, salt and black pepper, stirring constantly over high heat, allowing a crust to form on the bottom of the pan.

■ Add the water and stir the mixture, scraping the bottom to incorporate the browned crust. Add the bread crumbs and stir. The consistency should be like a thick stew. Add more water as needed. Cover, reduce the heat to very low and cook for 15 minutes. Set it aside to cool.

■ Preheat the oven to 400°F. Cut each piece of the dough into 9 pieces. Using a rolling pin on a floured surface, roll out each piece of pastry into a rectangle shape with rounded edges. Spread a large spoonful of the cooled meat mixture over one side of the dough, leaving at least a ½- to ¾-inch border on the outside edge. Using your finger, paint water around the border. Fold the other side of the dough over, and roll and crimp the edges. Lightly press a floured fork around the edge of the patty.

■ Place the patty onto a cookie sheet and repeat the procedure with the remaining dough. The patties may be covered in plastic and frozen at this point for later use. Brush each patty with the egg wash and bake for 20 minutes, or until the patties begin to turn a golden color.

NOTE—Serve as appetizers by making them miniature size.

VEGETABLE PATTIES

MAKES 18 PATTIES (6 TO 9 SERVINGS; 2 PER PERSON FOR LUNCH)

Vegetable patties are not the ubiquitous "patty" known to Jamaicans. But over recent years, they've become popular throughout Jamaica. The fillings vary greatly among cooks, so be sure to use poetic license when creating your own.

FOR THE PASTRY
2½ cups all-purpose flour
½ teaspoon salt
¼ teaspoon baking powder
2 tablespoons curry powder
½ cup butter (1 stick)
¾ cup ice-cold water

FOR THE FILLING
1 tablespoon vegetable oil
2 cloves garlic, minced
1 small yellow onion, finely chopped
2 teaspoons curry powder
1 pound pumpkin, peeled and chopped
   (about 2½ cups)
1½ cups water
¼ head cabbage, shredded (about
   1½ cups)
1 medium-size potato, diced
1 carrot, diced
½ chocho (chayote), peeled, pitted and
   diced (optional)
1 whole Scotch bonnet pepper
   (green recommended)
¾ teaspoon salt
½ teaspoon freshly ground black pepper

FOR THE EGG WASH
1 egg, beaten with 1 teaspoon water

A popular route between Ocho Rios and Kingston is Fern Gully (a four-mile expanse of road that was originally a riverbed), where enormous walls of vegetation feature over six hundred species of the finest varieties of ferns in all shapes and sizes. Along the journey is a roadside food stop known as Faith's Pen, a fast-food "service station," Jamaican style. What started as a congregation of roadside huts has been organized by the government into a row of neat wooden structures with colorful signs announcing their names and specialties such as Ackee and Salt Fish and Jerk Chicken. It is home to the often-mentioned Ragamuffin "Roots Tonic" juice bar, a fastidiously clean operation complete with fresh juice, sex tonics and a good collection of reggae dub music.

At Rose's Hot Spot, a Rastaman quietly and methodically prepares and cooks incredible vegetable patties. Hopefully, he'd approve of the following approximation, which bakes rather than fries the patties.

■ To make the pastry, combine the flour, salt, baking powder and curry powder in a large mixing bowl. Cut the butter into small pieces and add to the bowl. Working quickly and using your fingertips, squeeze the flour mixture and butter together and toss it by scooping under the mixture with both hands. When the mixture resembles a very coarse meal, add the water to the bowl.

■ With floured hands, mix and squeeze the dough just until it forms a ball. Knead it once or twice to combine it fully (the less kneading, the better). Separate the dough into 2 pieces, flattening each into a thick pancake; wrap the pieces in plastic, and set them in the refrigerator to chill for at least 15 minutes. (The dough will keep in the refrigerator up to 5 days. Remove it from the refrigerator 30 minutes before using it.)

■ For the filling, heat the oil in a large skillet over medium heat. Add the garlic and onion, stirring constantly for 30 seconds. Add the curry powder and cook for 2 minutes, continuing to stir and scrape the bottom of the pan. (Do not burn!)

■ Add the pumpkin and ¾ cup of the water and blend it well with the curry mixture. Cover the skillet and reduce the heat to low. Simmer gently for 10 to 15 minutes, or until the pumpkin is soft enough to mash.

■ Meanwhile, in a pot, add the cabbage and enough water to cover. Bring to a boil over high heat and cook for 3 minutes. Drain completely and set aside.

■ Crush the pumpkin until smooth, add the remaining ¾ cup water and stir. Add the cabbage, potato, carrot, chocho, Scotch bonnet pepper, salt and black pepper. Cover and simmer for 10 minutes. Remove the vegetable mixture from the skillet and place in a bowl. Let it cool. (It can be made ahead and will keep in the refrigerator, covered, for up to 5 days.) Remove the Scotch bonnet pepper before using.

■ Preheat the oven to 400°F. Cut each piece of the dough into 9 pieces. Using a rolling pin on a floured surface, roll out each piece of pastry into a rectangle shape with rounded edges. Spread a large spoonful of the cooled vegetable mixture over one side of the dough, leaving at least a ½-inch border on the outside edge. Using your finger, paint water around the border. Fold the other side of the dough over, and roll and crimp the edges. Lightly press a floured fork around the edge of the patty.

■ Place onto a cookie sheet and repeat the procedure with the remaining dough. (The patties may be covered in plastic and frozen at this point for later use.) Brush each patty with the egg wash and bake for 20 minutes, or until the patties begin to turn a golden color.

NOTE—Serve as appetizers by making them miniature size.

JOHNNY CAKES

MAKES 6 TO 8 CAKES (4 TO 6 SERVINGS)

Eaten with a traditional breakfast such as Ackee and Salt Fish, these cakes, originally called "Journey Cakes," are served with meat and seafood on many Caribbean islands.

2 cups all-purpose flour
2 teaspoons baking powder
½ teaspoon salt
2 tablespoons butter
¼ cup water, approximately
1 cup vegetable oil

■ In a large bowl, sift together the flour, baking powder and salt. Using your fingertips, rub in the butter. Add just enough water to achieve a stiff, smooth dough. Shape the cakes into 2-inch-wide discs.

■ Heat the oil in a large skillet over high heat until it is very hot. Fry the cakes in the hot oil until they are brown on both sides, 5 to 7 minutes.

DUMPLINGS

FLOUR DUMPLINGS MAKES 6 ROUND "FOOD" DUMPLINGS
OR ENOUGH SPINNERS FOR 1 POT OF SOUP

CORNMEAL DUMPLINGS MAKES EIGHT 2-INCH-ROUND DUMPLINGS
(ENOUGH FOR 1 POT OF SOUP)

Jamaicans take their dumplings very seriously! There are "spinners," small oblong ones that are served in soups and stews. Larger round dumplings are boiled and served as "food" alongside a main dish. Fufu is a type of dumpling made of any starchy food, such as green banana, yam, corn or cassava, and served in stews or as a dish by the same name. Johnny Cakes are a fried version of a dumpling.

Some cooks use baking soda to lighten the dumpling and others don't. Once again, it's up to your personal preference, so the recipe here is just a basic guideline.

There are no cooking directions for these two dumpling recipes because more specific instructions are provided elsewhere. They are called for in other recipes throughout the book, such as Red Pea Soup (page 57) and Pumpkin Soup (page 51).

FLOUR DUMPLINGS
1 cup all-purpose flour
¼ teaspoon salt
⅓ cup water

CORNMEAL DUMPLINGS
1 cup coarse cornmeal
¼ cup all-purpose flour
½ teaspoon salt
½ cup water, approximately

▧ In a medium-size bowl, combine the flour and salt. Stir in the water to distribute it evenly into the flour. With your hands, knead it to form a soft and smooth dough.

▧ In a medium-size bowl, combine the cornmeal, flour and salt. Stir in the water (adding more or less as needed) to distribute evenly into the cornmeal-flour mixture. With your hands, knead it to form a soft and smooth dough.

FESTIVAL

MAKES 8 SERVINGS

Festival is a relative newcomer to Jamaican cooking. Not until about twenty-five years ago did it begin to pop up at Hellshire Beach, where local vendors sell it with fried fish. It's similar to a Johnny Cake except for its shape and slightly sweet flavor. It is one of the few additional menu offerings along with jerk at the Boston Beach jerk pits and other larger jerk centers. The crispy sweetened cornmeal is a great foil for the spicy jerk meat.

1 cup all-purpose flour
¾ cup coarse cornmeal
2 tablespoons sugar
½ teaspoon salt
1 teaspoon baking powder
⅛ teaspoon ground allspice
   (dry pimento berries)
1 teaspoon vanilla
¾ cup milk
2 cups vegetable oil

▨ In a large bowl, mix together the flour, cornmeal, sugar, salt, baking powder and allspice. In another bowl, combine the vanilla and milk. Slowly stir the milk mixture into the flour mixture to achieve a thick batter. Turn the batter onto a floured surface, knead the dough lightly and form it into a log shape. Divide it into 8 pieces. With floured hands, roll each piece into a 4-inch-long sausage shape.

▨ Heat the oil in a large, deep skillet over high heat until it is very hot. Fry the dough, turning each piece until golden brown all over, 5 to 6 minutes. Drain on paper towels before serving.

CODFISH FRITTERS (STAMP AND GO)

MAKES 12 TO 16 FRITTERS (4 TO 6 SERVINGS)

Stamp and Go is up there with jerk pork as one of Jamaica's early fast foods. These fritters were a common roadside snack at the turn of the twentieth century. They make great spicy and crispy cocktail snacks that can be served with a chutney or cocktail sauce. They can be fried in advance and reheated in a 350°F oven for 10 minutes. Or you can microwave them for 1 minute.

½ pound salt cod
1 cup all-purpose flour
1 cup coarse cornmeal
1 teaspoon baking powder
½ teaspoon salt
¼ teaspoon freshly ground black pepper
¼ cup plus 2 tablespoons vegetable oil
2 tablespoons minced onion
2 whole scallions, finely chopped
1 clove garlic, minced
¼ sweet green or red pepper, finely chopped
½ Scotch bonnet pepper (any color), seeded and minced
1 small tomato, finely chopped
½ teaspoon dried thyme
1 cup water (or more)

■ Soak the cod for 2 days in enough water to cover, changing the water each day. Rinse well and steam it until cooked through, about 5 minutes. Flake and set it aside.

■ In a large bowl, combine the flour, cornmeal, baking powder, salt and black pepper.

■ Heat 2 tablespoons of the oil in a medium-size skillet and cook the onion, scallions, garlic, sweet pepper, Scotch bonnet pepper and tomato, stirring, for 2 minutes. Add the codfish and thyme to the pan and stir it to combine.

■ Add the cooked vegetables to the flour mixture and pour in the water, stirring until you have a slightly thick mixture which resembles pancake batter. (Add more water if it's too thick.)

■ Heat the remaining ¼ cup oil in a large skillet until it is very hot. Drop spoonfuls of the batter into the hot oil. Allow them to cook until bubbles form on the top, about 1½ minutes. Flip them over and continue to cook until the fritters are golden brown on both sides. Blot off the oil with paper and serve the fritters immediately with sauce.

NOTE—These can be fried in advance and reheated in a 350°F oven for 10 minutes. Or you can microwave them for 1 minute.

CORNMEAL FRITTERS

MAKES 12 FRITTERS (6 SERVINGS)

These savory morsels complement many vegetarian entrées such as Quick-Fried Cabbage (page 38). The spice of the pepper combines with the sweetness of the coconut milk for a clean and complex, yet salt-free, flavor. Try them as appetizers topped with a spoonful of Pawpaw Pepper Sauce (page 92) or Mango Chutney (page 91).

2 cups coarse or yellow cornmeal
1 teaspoon baking powder
2¼ cups coconut milk
1 onion, finely chopped
3 whole scallions, finely chopped
½ Scotch bonnet pepper (any color), seeded and minced, or ½ teaspoon hot sauce
½ cup vegetable oil

◾ In a medium-size bowl, mix together the cornmeal and baking powder. Add the coconut milk and stir until the batter is smooth. Add the onion, scallions and Scotch bonnet pepper, and stir the mixture until well combined. The batter should be moist yet firm enough to form into 2-inch patties with your hands. Add more cornmeal or liquid (coconut milk or water) if needed. (Rinse your hands with cold water before forming the patties so the batter doesn't stick to your hands.)

◾ In a large skillet, heat the oil until it is very hot. Carefully place the patties into the skillet while lightly shaking the pan to keep them from sticking. Fry in batches until golden on both sides, about 3 minutes per side, using more oil if needed. Remove the fritters and drain them on paper. Serve while still hot.

NOTE—These can be fried in advance and reheated in a 350°F oven for 10 minutes. Or you can microwave them for 1 minute.

QUICK-FRIED CABBAGE

MAKES 6 SERVINGS

Serve this alongside Cornmeal Fritters (page 39) and fresh Limeade (page 110) for a light vegetarian lunch or supper. The small tender cabbages found in Jamaica bear little resemblance to our large sturdy variety, but the flavor combination is still delicate and satisfying. This is an all-time favorite cabbage dish.

1 medium-size head cabbage (about 3 pounds)
¼ cup vegetable oil
1 small onion, thinly sliced (1 cup)
1 scallion, sliced
½ sweet green or red pepper, chopped
1 tomato, chopped (about ½ cup)
2 sprigs fresh thyme or 1½ teaspoons dried
1 teaspoon salt (optional)
1 whole Scotch bonnet pepper (any color)

■ Peel off the tough outer leaves of the cabbage and remove the inner core. Shred what remains and set it aside.

■ Heat the oil in a large skillet over medium-high heat until hot. Add the onion, scallion, sweet pepper and tomato. Raise the heat to high and cook until the vegetables have softened, about 5 minutes. Stir in the thyme, salt and Scotch bonnet pepper. Add all of the cabbage to the pan and stir to combine it with the onion mixture. Cover and reduce the heat to medium-low. Cook for 10 minutes, stirring occasionally. The recipe can be prepared in advance to this stage.

■ Remove the cover and continue to cook until the cabbage is tender but not too soft, about 5 minutes. Remove the hot pepper and thyme sprigs before serving.

VARIATION—This dish can also be prepared with carrots, which will make it sweeter and even more wholesome and colorful. Add ½ to 1 cup of shredded carrots to the skillet with the cabbage.

TURNED CORNMEAL

This versatile preparation is similar to Italian polenta. It can be eaten on its own, or it pairs nicely with any well-sauced dish. If you're lucky enough to have leftovers, slice and fry it as a tasty side for your morning eggs.

2 tablespoons vegetable oil
1 onion, finely chopped (about 1 cup)
3 whole scallions, finely sliced
1 tomato, chopped (about ½ cup)
¼ sweet green or red pepper, seeded and chopped
3 okra, sliced (about ¼ cup) (optional)
4 cups coconut milk
2 cups coarse cornmeal
1 teaspoon salt
½ teaspoon freshly ground black pepper
¼ Scotch bonnet pepper (any color), seeded and minced
¼ teaspoon dried thyme

▪ In a medium-size skillet, heat the oil over medium-high heat until it is very hot. Add the onion, scallions, tomato, sweet pepper and okra. Cook, stirring, until well blended and slightly dry, about 2 minutes. Remove from the heat.

▪ In a thick-bottomed saucepan, heat the coconut milk over low heat. Add the cornmeal, cooked vegetables, salt, black pepper, Scotch bonnet pepper and thyme. Cook for 20 minutes, turning frequently with a large, strong utensil.

▪ If serving immediately, spoon the cornmeal directly onto the plates. Otherwise, place the mixture in a serving dish and form it into a mold. When you are ready to serve, cut it into wedges.

▪ A simpler version of this recipe from a Jamaican friend goes like this: Fry an onion with a likkle wata and trow in de kahnmeal of 1 pownd. Turn and turn adding wata, 1 pint and a likkle.

RICE AND PEAS

MAKES 6 SERVINGS

Every Jamaican household, rich or poor, serves this nutritionally complete one-pot meal. It's the backbone of this island's cuisine, hence its moniker, "Jamaica Coat of Arms." Along with fried plantains, it's a Sunday lunch staple, yet for my money it's a perfect choice all by itself for any meal any day. This basic recipe has many variations according to personal tradition. I prefer not to use Scotch bonnet pepper, keeping it as a sweet, smooth complement to the robustly spiced dishes.

½ pound dried red peas (kidney beans) or
  small red beans (1 cup)
6 to 8 cups coconut milk
1 teaspoon freshly ground black pepper
2 whole scallions, crushed
2 sprigs fresh thyme or 1½ teaspoons dried
2 cups uncooked long-grain white rice
2 teaspoons salt

▨ Wash the beans thoroughly and place them in a medium-size saucepan with the coconut milk, black pepper, scallions and thyme. Bring to a boil over high heat, then reduce the heat to low, cover and simmer for 1 to 2 hours, or until the beans are almost tender (adding water as needed to keep the beans covered). Remove the thyme (if using whole sprigs) and scallions. Add the rice and salt. If necessary, add more water so that the liquid is 1 inch above the rice. Bring it to a boil over high heat, then reduce the heat, cover and simmer for 20 minutes. Fluff it with a fork. The grains of rice should easily separate and not be mushy.

CALLALOO

MAKES 6 SERVINGS AS A SIDE DISH

This abundant, leafy green has a firmer texture and fuller flavor (not bitter) than spinach. It is the main ingredient in Pepperpot Soup (page 54) and can be found in callaloo loaf at patty shops. Mineral-rich callaloo is another staple vegetable in every Jamaican's diet.

2 pounds callaloo (see Note)
1 tablespoon cooking oil
1 tablespoon butter
1 onion, chopped
3 whole scallions, chopped
1 sprig fresh thyme or ½ teaspoon dried
½ teaspoon salt
½ teaspoon freshly ground black pepper
⅓ cup water

▧ Remove the small branches with leaves from the main stem and submerge the callaloo into a bowl of cold water. Let soak for a minute and remove, discarding the water. Repeat 2 more times. Finely chop the leaves and branches and set aside.

▧ Heat the oil and butter in a medium-size skillet over medium heat until the butter is melted. Add the onion and scallions, stirring until the onion begins to soften, about 2 minutes. Add the callaloo, thyme, salt and black pepper. Mix all of the ingredients together, add the water and cover. Cook over medium heat until the stems are tender, about 8 minutes.

NOTE—Swiss chard or mustard greens are suitable substitutes for this dish. Spinach can become too mushy.

PUMPKIN VEGETABLE CURRY STEW

MAKES 6 SERVINGS

This stew is an excellent vegetarian main dish, and the pumpkin gives you a large dose of beta-carotene for a boost to the immune system. Serve it with Rice and Peas (page 40) and chutney.

3 tablespoons vegetable oil
1 onion, finely chopped
2 cloves garlic, minced
2 tablespoons curry powder
½ teaspoon cinnamon
½ teaspoon ground ginger
1 teaspoon salt (optional)
½ teaspoon freshly ground black pepper
2 tomatoes, chopped
⅔ cup water
1 pound pumpkin, peeled and chopped
1 carrot, sliced
1 potato, chopped
1 green banana or Irish potato, chopped
1 whole Scotch bonnet pepper
   (green recommended)

■ Heat the oil in a large skillet over medium-high heat. Add the onion and cook, stirring, for 2 minutes. Add the garlic and cook 1 minute more. Add the curry powder, cinnamon, ginger, salt and black pepper and cook, stirring, for 2 minutes. Add the tomatoes and stir until it is a thick, relishlike sauce.

■ Add the water, scraping the bottom of the pan to incorporate all the flavors. Add the pumpkin, carrot, potato, green banana and Scotch bonnet pepper. Raise the heat to high and bring to a boil while gently blending the ingredients together. Cover, reduce the heat to medium-low and simmer, stirring a couple of times, until the vegetables are tender, about 20 minutes. Remove the Scotch bonnet pepper before serving.

AVOCADO SALAD

MAKES 6 SERVINGS

The avocado, or "pear" as it's known in Jamaica, has been eaten since 1492 when Christopher Columbus came to the Caribbean. It's been called "poor man's butter" and today remains a favorite vegetable, most often just served peeled and sliced as a side to the morning meal or with a sweet snack.

3 cups shredded lettuce
3 ripe avocados
Juice of 1 lime
1 teaspoon salt
1 small onion, finely sliced
2 small tomatoes, quartered
½ teaspoon ground white pepper or black pepper

■ Spread out the lettuce on a platter. Peel and slice the avocados, discarding the pits, and place the slices in a bowl. Toss the avocado slices with the lime juice and salt. Arrange the pieces evenly over the lettuce. Place the onion and tomatoes over the top. Sprinkle the pepper on top.

STUFFED AND BAKED CHOCHOS

MAKES 4 SERVINGS OR 8 AS A SIDE DISH

The pear shape of chocho makes it ideal for stuffing. The naturally subtle-tasting flesh, which is similar to cucumber, works well with a variety of other foods as it absorbs any flavor into its own. Don't hesitate to experiment with your own stuffing. These make a great lunch, light supper or side dish with a larger meal.

4 chochos (chayote) or cucumbers
½ pound ground beef
1 small onion, finely chopped
1 clove garlic, minced
½ Scotch bonnet pepper (any color), seeded and minced
½ teaspoon dried thyme
1 tablespoon oil
1 tablespoon butter
¼ cup plain bread crumbs (preferably fresh)
¾ cup grated white Cheddar cheese
½ teaspoon Worcestershire sauce
½ teaspoon salt
¼ teaspoon freshly ground black pepper

■ In a large pot of boiling water, cook the chochos until they are tender, about 20 minutes. Meanwhile, in a large bowl, combine the beef, onion, garlic, Scotch bonnet pepper and thyme. Refrigerate until needed.

■ Remove the chochos from the boiling water and set aside. When they are cool enough to handle, cut each one in half and remove the pits. Scoop out some of the flesh from each half by scoring it first with a small, sharp knife and then lifting it out with the edge of a spoon. Be sure to leave enough flesh around the skins to keep them sturdy. Dice the flesh and put it aside in a small bowl. Preheat the oven to 400°F.

■ In a large skillet, heat the oil and butter until very hot. Add the meat mixture and cook until browned, 8 to 10 minutes. Clean the bowl and set it aside. Add the diced chocho to the pan and cook it for 2 minutes. Return the meat and chocho mixture to the bowl. Add the bread crumbs, ½ cup of the cheese, Worcestershire sauce, salt and black pepper and mix well.

■ Spoon a large scoop of filling into each chocho half. Place the pieces next to each other in a large ovenproof pan. Put any leftover stuffing into a small ovenproof baking dish. Sprinkle the remaining ¼ cup of cheese on the chocho halves. Bake for 10 to 15 minutes.

VARIATION—For a vegetarian version of this dish, substitute 1 cup cooked brown rice for the meat. Cucumbers can be used in place of chochos. Rinse them well and halve them lengthwise. Complete as directed, except boil them for 5 to 10 minutes instead of 20.

PUMPKIN SOUP

MAKES 6 TO 8 SERVINGS

My fondest childhood memory of Jamaican food is pumpkin soup. Spinners (small, elongated dumplings) swimming in the nourishing orange broth make this simple soup a treasure trove. Yellow or white yams can be used instead of or in addition to spinners. Unfortunately, many Jamaicans now opt for packaged seasoning over bones and the slow-simmering soup pot. What a shame! Serve as a light meal or a dinner starter.

½ pound pig's tail, salted (optional)
3 pounds beef with bone, such as short ribs or shin
2 pounds pumpkin, peeled and cubed
10 cups water
3 whole scallions, crushed
2 cloves garlic, crushed
1 whole Scotch bonnet pepper, plus 2 slices (any color)
1 sprig fresh thyme or 1 teaspoon dried
1½ teaspoons salt (optional)
½ teaspoon freshly ground black pepper
½ pound yellow or white yam, peeled and chopped (optional)

FOR THE SPINNERS
1¼ cups all-purpose flour
¼ teaspoon salt
½ cup water

■ If you are using a pig's tail, soak it in two 10-minute water baths and rinse. Place it in a large soup pot along with the beef, pumpkin and water. Bring to a boil, reduce the heat to medium-low and simmer until the pumpkin has dissolved and the beef is tender, about 1½ hours.

■ Meanwhile, to prepare the spinners, in a medium-size bowl, sift together the flour and salt. Add the water and blend with a wooden spoon until a ball is formed. Flour your hands and knead slightly to form a soft dough. Add more flour if the dough is too sticky. Cover and set aside.

When the meat is tender, remove it from the pot. Separate the meat from the bones, chop it and return it to the pot. Bring to a brisk simmer over medium heat and add the scallions, garlic, Scotch bonnet pepper, thyme, salt (if not using pig's tail) and black pepper. If using, place the yam in the pot.

Bring to a simmer again. Form the spinners by rolling small pieces of dough between your floured palms to form 1-inch-long oblong shapes. Drop the spinners into the soup one at a time. Stir gently to prevent them from sticking to the bottom. Continue to cook the soup for 15 minutes. Remove the whole Scotch bonnet pepper before serving.

PEPPERPOT SOUP

MAKES 6 TO 8 SERVINGS

This soup is dominated by the mineral-rich leafy green known as callaloo, which is similar to spinach. It has its origin with the Arawak Indians, who were the first known inhabitants of Jamaica. Over the years it's evolved from a callaloo-based stew to more of a soup dish using a vast array of vegetables. Different recipes derive their rich flavor bases from either smoked pork, shrimp, crab or salt cod, depending on the availability of ingredients or taste preference.

½ pound callaloo or spinach, chopped
½ pound kale, chopped
½ pound smoked pork, such as ham hocks
½ pound beef with bones, such as shin
10 okra, chopped
1 tomato, chopped
1 whole Scotch bonnet pepper (green recommended)
10 cups water
5 whole scallions, chopped
3 cloves garlic, minced
2 sprigs fresh thyme or 1½ teaspoons dried
2 teaspoons salt
¾ teaspoon freshly ground black pepper
1 to 4 slices Scotch bonnet pepper (any color)
1 chocho (chayote), peeled, pitted and chopped,
  or 1 cucumber, peeled and chopped
½ pound yellow yam, peeled and chopped (optional)
2 cups fresh or canned coconut milk

FOR THE DUMPLINGS
1¼ cups all-purpose flour
½ teaspoon salt
⅓ cup water

■ Wash the callaloo or spinach and kale thoroughly by submerging in 2 to 3 different cold water baths. Lift the greens out first, then discard the water. Place the greens in a large soup pot (a Dutch oven is ideal) along with the pork, beef, okra, tomato, whole Scotch bonnet pepper and water. Bring to a boil, reduce the heat to medium-low and partially cover. Simmer for 1½ hours.

■ Remove the whole Scotch bonnet pepper. Take out the pork and beef from the pot and separate the meat from the bone and fat. Chop the meat and return it to the pot. Add the scallions, garlic, thyme, salt, black pepper, sliced Scotch bonnet pepper, chocho, yam and coconut milk. Cook for 30 minutes, adding water if needed for a proper soup consistency.

To prepare the dumplings, in a medium bowl, sift together the flour and salt. Add the water and blend with a wooden spoon until a ball is formed. Flour your hands and knead slightly to form a soft dough. Form it into flat round shapes (will make 8 to 10). Cook them in boiling water for 15 minutes. Serve the soup piping hot with a dumpling in each bowl.

NOTE—Don't hesitate to use other vegetables, such as pumpkin, sweet pepper, cabbage or Irish potatoes, as replacements or additions if you have any on hand.

RED PEA SOUP

Red peas are what folks outside Jamaica know as kidney beans. This is one of the most popular soups in Jamaica and it's certainly economical. It varies from cook to cook but has the same basic elements in common, often distinguished by a smoked meat. This is a hearty soup, suitable as a complete meal in itself, yet it also makes a nice starter for a large meal. You may make substitutions for the recommended vegetables (yams for potatoes, for example). Vegetarians may omit the ham hock and beef.

1 pound dried red peas (kidney beans)
2 pounds soup beef with bones
1 ham hock or other smoked pork
11 cups water
1 carrot, finely chopped
1 chocho (chayote), peeled, pitted and chopped,
   or 1 cucumber, peeled, seeded and chopped
1 Irish potato, peeled and chopped
1 whole Scotch bonnet pepper (green recommended)
2 slices Scotch bonnet pepper (any color)
3 cloves garlic
3 whole scallions
1 sprig fresh thyme or 1 teaspoon dried
2 teaspoons salt
½ teaspoon freshly ground black pepper

FOR THE SPINNERS
1¼ cups all-purpose flour
¼ teaspoon salt
½ cup water

■ Rinse the red peas, beef and ham hock separately and place them in a large soup pot with 10 cups of the water. Bring to a boil over high heat. Reduce the heat to medium-low and partially cover the pot. Cook at a brisk simmer until the peas are soft and the meat is tender, about 2 hours.

■ Meanwhile, to prepare the spinners, in a medium-size bowl, sift together the flour and salt. Add the ½ cup of water and blend with a wooden spoon until a ball is formed. Flour your hands and knead slightly to form a soft dough. Add more flour if it is too sticky. Cover and set aside.

▓ Remove the beef and pork from the pan and set aside. With the back of a spoon, mash some of the peas in the soup pot.

▓ Add the carrot, chocho, potato, whole and sliced Scotch bonnet peppers, garlic, scallions, thyme, salt, black pepper and remaining 1 cup of water. Cook for 30 minutes more. With 15 minutes of cooking time left, form the spinners by rolling small pieces of dough between your floured palms to form 1-inch-long oblong shapes. Drop into the soup one at a time. Stir gently to prevent the spinners from sticking to the bottom.

▓ Remove the meat from the bones of the beef and pork. Discard the bones, chop the meat into small pieces and return it to the soup pot. Remove the whole Scotch bonnet pepper, scallions and thyme sprig (if using). Serve immediately or refrigerate it until needed. Blend in 1 cup more water if you are reheating it.

VARIATIONS—For an even heartier soup, drop in spinners with 20 minutes cooking time left. If you are reheating the soup, be careful that the spinners don't stick to the bottom of the pan.

OXTAIL SOUP

MAKES 6 TO 8 SERVINGS

The oxtail makes a rich and intensely flavored soup. Any beef lover will appreciate it.

½ pound oxtail
⅓ cup large dry white beans (lima or broad)
10 cups water
½ yam, peeled and chopped (about ½ pound)
1 chocho (chayote), peeled, pitted and chopped, or 1 cucumber, peeled, seeded and chopped
1 tomato, chopped
2 whole scallions, sliced
1 clove garlic, minced
1 sprig fresh thyme or 1 teaspoon dried
2 teaspoons salt
½ teaspoon freshly ground black pepper
1 whole Scotch bonnet pepper (any color)

FOR THE SPINNERS
1¼ cups all-purpose flour
¼ teaspoon salt
¼ cup water

■ Wash the oxtail in water and place it in a large soup pot along with the beans and water. Bring to a boil over high heat, then reduce the heat to medium-low and simmer, partially covered, for 2 hours. Add the yam, chocho, tomato, scallions, garlic, thyme, salt, black pepper and Scotch bonnet pepper. Simmer for 45 minutes more.

■ For the spinners, combine the flour, salt and water. Knead the dough until you have a smooth, sticky ball. With 20 minutes left of cooking time, add the spinners one at a time to the soup. Roll a small piece between the palms of your hands, forming a narrow, oval shape, and drop into the soup. Simmer for 20 minutes. Remove the Scotch bonnet pepper before serving.

FISH TEA

MAKES 6 SERVINGS

The word "tea" is often used in Jamaica to describe different types of hot beverages, no doubt due to the British influence on the local language.

You'll find fish tea in seaside places where items like steamed or roasted fish are served. Depending on the local fish, the soup differs slightly from region to region. The dense-fleshed turbot used on the south coast makes for a much creamier texture, while up north, snapper and parrot fish produce a lighter and thinner broth.

2 pounds fish with head and bones
2 green bananas or Irish potatoes, chopped
½ pound pumpkin, peeled and diced
1 chocho (chayote), peeled, pitted and chopped, or 1 cucumber, peeled, seeded and chopped
1 potato, peeled and chopped
¼ pound okra, sliced
3 whole scallions
1 teaspoon dried thyme
1 whole Scotch bonnet pepper (any color)
½ teaspoon salt
½ teaspoon freshly ground black pepper
10 cups water

■ Place all of the ingredients in a large soup pot and bring to a boil over high heat. Reduce the heat to medium-low and simmer for 1 hour. Remove the Scotch bonnet pepper. Strain out the fish bones, if desired, before serving

MAIN
DISHES
AND
SAUCES

JERK CHICKEN

MAKES 6 TO 8 SERVINGS

For takeout at a roadside jerk stand, servings of this slow-cooked fast food come cleverly wrapped and placed in a white rectangular cardboard cake (charlotte) box. Spoon on some hot sauce, clamp down the lid, grab a napkin and you're ready to roll. Chop the meat before serving, bone and all, since half the fun is picking through the rubble for the prized meat. To serve the most proper guests, boned chicken thighs are quicker and easier. Serve as a light meal with Festival (page 31), Johnny Cakes (page 29) or hard dough bread.

5 bunches whole scallions, finely chopped
3 large cloves garlic, minced
3 Scotch bonnet peppers (any color), seeded and minced
2 sprigs fresh thyme or 2 tablespoons dried
¼ cup ground allspice (dry pimento berries)
2 tablespoons freshly ground black pepper
1½ tablespoons salt
1 cup water
5 pounds chicken thighs or 2 small whole chickens, cut into quarters (see Note)

▓ Combine all of the ingredients except the water and chicken in a large bowl. Mix well and add the water to form a loose paste.

▓ Reserve ½ cup of the sauce for a later use. Marinate the chicken in the remaining sauce for at least 1 hour or as long as 24 hours (the longer, the better). Turn the meat several times, mixing the sauce.

▓ Prepare an outdoor barbecue using plenty of coals. Meanwhile, soak small sticks or hardwood chips in water (mesquite conflicts with jerk's own flavor). When the coals have become gray and well ashed over, add the soaked wood to the fire.

■ Place the chicken on the grill and cover, leaving the vent holes open. Barbecue slowly—1½ to 2 hours, depending on the size of the pieces. Check the fire after 30 minutes, adding coal or wood as needed and being careful not to flame the fire. Baste every 30 minutes with the marinade. Turn the chicken several times as it cooks. The chicken is done when it is firm to the touch and slightly charred.

■ Remove the chicken from the fire and let it sit on a cutting board for 15 minutes. If you have a sharp cleaver, chop the meat into small pieces (bone and all); otherwise, leave each piece whole. Serve on a large platter doused with the reserved jerk sauce.

NOTE—For boneless chicken thighs (breasts tend to dry out), use the same preparation, but change the barbecue time to 30 or 40 minutes. Cut into large bite-size pieces.

JERK PORK

Boasting a high number of "special" ingredients carries some weight among the authorities, yet I have equal results with my simple, essential version. All you need is a grill with a tight-fitting lid, ice-cold Red Stripe beer and a thumping reggae beat. Everyone will be happy. Serve it with plenty of extra sauce and roast yam or bread or Festival (page 31).

5 bunches scallions, finely chopped
3 large cloves garlic, minced
3 Scotch bonnet peppers (any color), minced
2 large sprigs fresh thyme or 2 tablespoons dried
¼ cup ground allspice (dry pimento berries)
2 tablespoons freshly ground black pepper
1½ tablespoons salt
1 cup water
6 to 8 pounds pork shoulder, boned and butterflied

■ Combine all of the ingredients except the water and pork in a large bowl. Mix well and add enough water to form a loose paste.

■ Put 2½ cups of the sauce in another large bowl and add the pork. (Reserve the remaining sauce for serving.) Spread the sauce all over the meat and marinate, refrigerated, for at least 1 hour or as long as 24 hours (the longer, the better), turning occasionally.

■ Prepare an outdoor barbecue as usual, using plenty of coals. Meanwhile, soak small sticks or hardwood chips in water for 30 minutes. Pimento is preferred, but any wood without a strong flavor is fine. (Mesquite conflicts with jerk's own flavor.) When the coals have become gray and well ashed over, add the soaked wood.

■ Place the meat on the grill and cover, leaving the vent holes slightly open. The pork should cook very slowly for about 2½ hours. Check the fire after 1 hour and add a few coals and wood as needed. Baste every 30 minutes with the marinade. Turn the meat several times as it cooks. The meat is cooked when it is firm to the touch and slightly charred.

Remove the meat from the fire and let it sit on a cutting board for 15 minutes with foil loosely placed on top. Using a cleaver, chop the meat into bite-size pieces. Serve on a large platter, doused with some of the reserved jerk sauce.

VARIATION—Any leftover meat can be shredded and mixed with jerk sauce and served on a sandwich or crackers for appetizers.

CURRY CHICKEN

MAKES 6 TO 8 SERVINGS

Chicken became the meat of choice for the English in their curry dishes, although the East Indians, who brought the style with them, used goat. Today, curry is an essential flavor and preparation style in Jamaican cooking. Commercial curry powder varies greatly in quality and flavor. It loses its punch if allowed to sit in the cupboard too long. For purists, making the powder from fresh spices is the best. Serve this with white rice and chutney. This dish is even better the next day. Hopefully there will be leftovers.

Two 3-pound chickens
2 limes, juice and grated rind
½ cup vegetable oil
2 tablespoons butter (optional)
3 small onions, chopped
4 cloves garlic, minced
4 tablespoons curry powder
3 tomatoes, chopped, or ¼ cup tomato sauce
1 Scotch bonnet pepper (any color), plus
   2 to 4 slices (any color)
2 teaspoons salt
¾ teaspoon freshly ground black pepper
4 cups water

■ Rinse the chickens with water and pat them dry with paper towels. Cut the chickens into serving pieces and place in a large bowl, reserving the backs, necks and wing tips for stock or another use. Juice the limes and add the juice to the chicken along with the grated lime rind, coating the chicken with the juice.

■ In a large skillet, heat ¼ cup of the oil and 1 tablespoon of the butter, if using, over high heat until very hot. Pat the chicken dry again and carefully add half of the pieces to the skillet. Fry on one side for 3 to 4 minutes, shaking and tilting the skillet a little to distribute the fat. Turn the chicken over and fry for 3 minutes more, or until golden brown. Remove the chicken to a large platter and set aside.

■ Pour out the old fat, wipe the skillet and add the remaining ¼ cup oil and 1 tablespoon butter, if using. Repeat the frying procedure with the remaining chicken pieces and then set aside.

■ Discard all but 2 tablespoons of oil, reduce the heat to medium and add the onions and garlic to the skillet. Cook, stirring, for 1 minute (be careful not to burn the garlic). Add the curry powder and fry for 1 more minute, scraping the bottom.

■ Add the tomatoes, whole Scotch bonnet pepper and slices, salt and black pepper. Stir thoroughly while scraping the bottom of the pan. Add the water and mix until well blended. Return the chicken to the pan. Bring it to a boil and reduce the heat to a simmer. Cover and cook for 45 minutes, or until the chicken is tender.

VARIATION—Add ½ cup of shredded coconut just before serving.

CHICKEN FRICASSEE

MAKES 6 TO 8 SERVINGS

This delicious and popular dish is intuitively prepared in several variations by Jamaicans. Don't confuse the rustic Jamaican style with the French, cream-based sauce. A few simple ingredients and a quick preparation result in a most unusual taste and a satisfying meal. Serve with white rice and Avocado Salad (page 47).

Two 3-pound chickens
2 limes, rinsed and quartered
1 teaspoon salt
½ teaspoon freshly ground black pepper
4 small yellow onions, thinly sliced
4 tomatoes, chopped
4 cloves garlic, minced
1 sprig fresh thyme or 1 teaspoon dried
1 whole Scotch bonnet pepper
  (green recommended)
1 to 3 slices Scotch bonnet pepper
  (red recommended)
¼ cup vegetable oil
2 cups water or chicken stock

▓ Rinse the chickens and pat them dry with paper towels. Cut the chickens into serving pieces. To make a quick broth, if desired, place the chicken backs, necks and wing tips into a small pot and cover with water. Bring to a boil, reduce the heat to low and simmer until needed.

▓ Place the other chicken pieces in a large bowl and squeeze the limes over them, coating each piece with juice. (Leave the lime rinds in the bowl.) Sprinkle on the salt and black pepper, add the onions, tomatoes, garlic, thyme and Scotch bonnet peppers, and mix well. Set aside to marinate for at least 15 minutes and up to an hour.

▓ In a large skillet, heat half of the oil over high heat until it is very hot. Fry half the pieces of chicken until golden on both sides, about 5 minutes per side. Remove the pieces from the pan and set aside on a large plate. Wipe out the old oil and add the remaining oil. Repeat the frying process with the rest of the chicken pieces. Remove the chicken from the pan and pour out the oil. Discard the lime rinds from the tomato mixture. Return the pan to medium-high heat, add all the chicken pieces and tomato mixture and cook, stirring, for 3 minutes. Blend in the water or chicken stock. Reduce the heat to medium-low, cover and simmer until the chicken is tender, 40 to 45 minutes. Remove the whole Scotch bonnet pepper. Serve the chicken with the sauce spooned over it.

BEEF STEW

MAKES 6 TO 8 SERVINGS

One of my favorite dishes and a classic dish in many cultures is beef stew, also known as stewed beef. Jamaicans might serve theirs with steamed rice and boiled green bananas. This is an easy recipe that requires minimal ingredients. This nonspicy version is friendly for everyone. But don't forget to have a fiery bottle of hot sauce on the table.

4 pounds stew beef without bones, such as chuck, well trimmed and cubed
1½ teaspoons salt
¼ teaspoon freshly ground black pepper
¼ cup vegetable oil
1 tablespoon butter (optional)
2 small onions, chopped
1 clove garlic, minced
½ sweet red pepper, seeded and finely chopped
1 tomato, chopped
2½ cups water
2 potatoes, cubed
3 carrots, sliced

■ Place the beef into a large bowl. Season it with ½ teaspoon of the salt and the black pepper. In a large skillet over high, heat the oil until it is very hot. (Keep a lid nearby for splattering oil.)

■ Carefully place some of the meat into the pan without crowding it. Fry for 4 minutes on each side to achieve a golden brown crust. Remove from the pan with a slotted or webbed spoon. Repeat the procedure with the remaining beef. Turn the heat down to low. (The pan should have a dark brown, not burnt, crust.)

■ Add the butter, if using. Turn the heat to medium. When the butter is melted, add the onions and garlic, stirring it constantly until it is dark golden, about 2 minutes. Add the sweet pepper and tomato, scraping the bottom of the pan with a spatula. Cook for 4 minutes until it is well blended and thickened.

■ Return the beef along with its juices to the pan. Mix well and add the water. Bring it to a boil over high heat, then cover and reduce the heat to low. Simmer until the meat is tender, 2½ hours. Add the potatoes, carrots and remaining 1 teaspoon of salt. Stir, cover, and cook for 30 more minutes.

VARIATION—For a spicier version, add a whole Scotch bonnet pepper along with the vegetables.

POT ROAST

MAKES 6 TO 8 SERVINGS

A little pamphlet I found in the Kingston library called *Cooking with Red Stripe* by Tony Gambrill places Jamaican pot roast in the same family as the classic Belgian dish carbonnade, where beer was used by Belgian peasants to tenderize less expensive cuts of beef. Here I use Jamaican Dragon Stout for an extra-rich sauce, but any beer will work perfectly well. Serve it heaped over buttered noodles.

4 to 5 pounds top round or other
  economical cut of beef
2 cloves garlic, minced
½ teaspoon dry mustard
½ teaspoon ground ginger
2 teaspoons salt
1 teaspoon freshly ground black pepper
¼ cup soy sauce
¼ cup vegetable oil
1 onion, finely chopped
2 tomatoes, chopped
12 ounces beer, preferably stout
4 potatoes, chopped
2 carrots, sliced

■ Bring the meat to room temperature, rinse thoroughly and pat dry with a paper towel. Combine the garlic, mustard, ginger, salt, black pepper and soy sauce. Spread the mixture on the meat and set aside to marinate, refrigerated, for 1 hour.

■ Heat the oil in a large Dutch oven over medium heat. Add the meat and cook until browned on all sides, being careful not to burn it. Add the onion and cook until it wilts and darkens, about 5 minutes. Add the tomatoes and cook, stirring, for 2 minutes. Add the beer. Raise the heat to high and bring to a boil, then reduce the heat to low and simmer for 2 to 3 hours, adding water as needed. Add the potatoes and carrots and cook, covered, until the vegetables are tender and the meat is easily cut, about 30 minutes.

VARIATION—Use whatever other root vegetables you have on hand, if desired.

FRIED FISH AND BAMMY

MAKES 2 SERVINGS

Gloria's Rendezvous in the easy haven of Port Royal at the entrance to Kingston harbor is famous for its fried fish and bammy. Port Royal used to be known, in the buccaneer days of the seventeenth century, as the "wickedest city in the world." On the streets at night townsfolk are casually grouped together, engaged in languorous activities like dominoes and jump rope.

While waiting for our fish, we usually stroll down to The Angler's Club bar for Red Stripes and bags of tiny, dried pepper shrimp. We wander back to Gloria's through the soft ocean breeze, beers in hand, past the community gardens and curbside fish ladies selling escovitch fish.

At home this can be almost as good with the freshest fish, hottest oil and most tolerantly nosed housemates. Serve with a pitcher of iced Limeade (page 110). Bammy, the original Arawak bread made from grated sweet cassava, is rarely homemade but obtained from bammy ladies who sell these flat, circular breads in packages on the roadside—they are served steamed or fried with fish.

Two ¾-pound whole fish, such as snapper or any mild-flavored fish, gutted, heads and tails left on
Juice of 1 lime
½ teaspoon salt
¼ teaspoon freshly ground black pepper
½ cup vegetable oil
4 bammy, soaked, or 4 Johnny Cakes (page 29)
4 slices sweet red pepper
6 slices onion

■ Rinse the fish thoroughly inside and out with water. Rub the lime juice all over the fish. Pat it dry with a paper towel. Slash each fish diagonally down to the bone, twice on each side. Season with the salt and black pepper.

In a large skillet, heat the oil over medium-high heat until it is very hot (almost smoking). Carefully place both of the fish in the pan and tilt the pan slightly to distribute the oil underneath the fish and prevent them from sticking. Cook until the fish are a deep golden brown, about 4 minutes. Using 2 spatulas, gently turn the fish and cook for 5 minutes more. Put the cooked fish onto a paper towel to drain off the fat.

In the same pan, fry the soaked bammy in the fish fat for 3 minutes per side. Remove from the pan and drain on paper towels. Serve the fish and bammy immediately, garnished with the sweet pepper and onion slices.

VARIATION: For escovitch fish, pour Pawpaw Pepper Sauce (page 92) over the fried fish. Refrigerate for up to 12 hours.

ACKEE AND SALT FISH

MAKES 6 TO 8 SERVINGS

Jamaica's national dish features the mild ackee fruit whose flesh resembles scrambled eggs in both taste and texture. It teams up beautifully with the salty, toothsome fish.

Jamaicans consume more ackee than any other Caribbean people. In fact, "Jamaica Poisoning" is a potentially lethal condition caused from eating an immature or overripe ackee.

It must be picked when the pod has turned red and is completely split open, exposing the black seed and yellow flesh (the edible part is known as the aril).

This dish is traditionally served at breakfast along with dumplings, Johnny Cakes (page 29) or other starchy foods.

½ pound salt cod, soaked in water to cover overnight, refrigerated
2 dozen ackee
3 tablespoons vegetable oil
1 onion, sliced
1 tomato, chopped
¼ teaspoon salt or to taste
½ teaspoon freshly ground black pepper
2 slices Scotch bonnet pepper (any color), seeded and minced (optional)

■ Drain and rinse the salt cod. Place it in a large pot of boiling fresh water and cook for 15 minutes. When cool, flake it into small pieces and set it aside.

■ Clean the ackee by removing the black seed and pink membrane found in the yellow crease of the flesh. Bring another large pot of water to a boil, add the cleaned ackee and cook for 5 minutes.

In a large skillet, heat the oil over medium-high heat. Add the onion and tomato and cook, stirring, until the onion softens, about 3 minutes. Add the salt cod, ackee, salt, black pepper and Scotch bonnet pepper, if using. To avoid breaking up the ackee, stir it gently until it is cooked through and the flavors are well blended, about 5 minutes.

VARIATION: You can substitute bacon for the salt cod or omit the salt cod altogether.

STEAMED FISH

MAKES 4 TO 6 SERVINGS

The tradition continues at Flo's number one fish and bammy shack in Hellshire Beach outside Kingston. Flo presides as her mother did before her. Her warm smile belies her feminine strength, which forms the backbone of Jamaican life. Working in an effortless unison, Flo and Carl (the chef) regulate the fire temperature and tend to the cooking. They freely share their methods, which are highly evolved yet simple in form.

Saturday and Sunday breakfast at Hellshire Beach is an old-time family activity for Kingstonians. Flo cooks to order. No yam? Extra pepper? No problem. Just pick your fresh fish and leave it to the masters. It's an all-in-one meal, served with yellow yam and the optional steamed bammy.

Two 2-pound or one 5-pound whole fish, such as red snapper
3 teaspoons salt
1 teaspoon freshly ground black pepper
12 cups water (more or less depending on the quantity of fish)
1½ pounds pumpkin, peeled and chopped (about 5 cups)
3 scallions, cut into 1-inch pieces
7 okra, cut into 1-inch pieces
3 slices Scotch bonnet pepper (any color)
1 large sprig fresh thyme or 2 teaspoons dried
Four ½-inch-wide slices peeled yellow yam
2 tablespoons butter
10 allspice berries (dry pimento berries) (optional)
4 bammy or dumplings (optional)

■ Rinse the fish and pat dry with paper towels. With a small, sharp knife, make 3 vertical slits across the flesh. Season both sides (rub inside the slit) with 1 teaspoon of the salt and the black pepper. Cover and set aside at room temperature.

■ Place the water and pumpkin in a large pot that has a snug-fitting lid. Bring to a boil over high heat and cook until the pumpkin becomes soft, about 30 minutes, crushing it with a large spoon against the side of the pot.

■ In a bowl, combine the scallions, okra, Scotch bonnet pepper and thyme. Set aside.

■ Add the yam to the pot and boil for 15 minutes more, continuing to crush the pumpkin. Add the scallion mixture and stir. Add the butter, the remaining 2 teaspoons of salt and allspice and stir to combine.

■ Gently place the fish into the pot (it should be barely covered with liquid). Spoon some broth over the top of the fish. Cover and cook briskly for 10 minutes per inch of fish (measured at the thickest part of the fish). Add the bammy, placing it next to the fish, alongside the yam, with 5 to 10 minutes of cooking time left.

■ Lift the fish onto a large platter. Place the yam and the bammy around it. Spoon the liquid over the fish. Serve steaming hot.

STEWED FISH

MAKES 6 SERVINGS

This lightly seasoned, boneless fish recipe is an excellent choice for kids and adults who don't like things too spicy! Serve with white rice and sliced tomatoes.

1½ pounds boneless fish fillet
1 lime
¾ teaspoon salt
¼ teaspoon ground white pepper
¼ teaspoon ground allspice (dry pimento berries)
3 whole scallions, sliced
½ small onion, thinly sliced
½ cup milk
1 tablespoon all-purpose flour
1 cup water
¼ teaspoon Worcestershire sauce
¼ cup vegetable oil

■ Rinse the fish and pat dry with paper towels. Cut the fish into 6 equal pieces and squeeze the lime over both sides of each piece. Sprinkle the salt, white pepper and allspice evenly over all sides of the fish and place on a large plate. Distribute the scallions and onion over the top of the fish, cover and let it season for 30 minutes.

■ Meanwhile, in a 2-cup pitcher or bowl, gradually mix 3 tablespoons of the milk into the flour to make a smooth paste. Add the remaining milk, water and Worcestershire sauce and blend until well combined. Set aside.

■ Heat the oil in a large skillet over medium-high heat until it is very hot. Place the fish, skin side up, along with the seasonings, into the hot oil. Cook on one side until golden brown, about 2 minutes. Turn each piece and cook until golden, about 1 minute more.

▥ Slowly add the flour-milk mixture to the pan, scraping the bottom with a heat-proof spatula. Reduce the heat to medium-low, turn the fish again and simmer gently, uncovered, until the sauce thickens, about 3 minutes. Cover and cook it for another 3 to 4 minutes, or until the fish is cooked through.

PEPPER SHRIMP

If you happen to be traveling in Jamaica in the Parish of St. Elizabeth near the town of Black River, be prepared to stop by the side of the road in Middle Quarters, where the shrimp ladies sell small bags of river shrimp cooked with Scotch bonnet pepper. Try this as blazingly hot as you can stand it with a cold drink not too far from your reach. This makes a great appetizer for a feisty crowd.

1 pound small shrimp, unpeeled with heads and tails left on
3 tablespoons salt
¼ cup water
4 Scotch bonnet peppers (any color), seeded and minced

■ Place the shrimp and salt in a medium-size saucepan and mix gently with your hands. Add the water. Distribute the minced Scotch bonnet peppers evenly over the shrimp. Over high heat, bring the shrimp to a boil, then cover the pan and cook for 4 minutes, stirring after each minute, or until the shrimp are pink and cooked through. Remove from the heat and chill before serving.

■ You can make this much less spicy by adding 1 whole Scotch bonnet pepper instead of 4 minced.

CURRY SHRIMP

MAKES 6 SERVINGS

This recipe is from Erryll, a.k.a. Float, a.k.a. Cock Upon the Water, a fisherman down in Bluefields on the south coast. The recipe is simply stated as follows: "Burn de curry in h'oil, add de seasoning, okra, shrimp and water. H'allow to cook far a short while." Eaten on a riverbank, after catching the shrimp and cooking it over an open fire, this is a true experience! Serve with rice and Mango Chutney (page 91).

3 tablespoons vegetable oil
2 tablespoons curry powder
1 medium-size onion, chopped
1 whole scallion, chopped
1 clove garlic, minced
3 tablespoons seeded and diced sweet red pepper
1 slice Scotch bonnet pepper (any color)
¼ teaspoon freshly ground black pepper
3 tablespoons tomato sauce or paste
1 cup water
1 cup sliced okra
1 pound medium-size shrimp, peeled and deveined

■ Heat the oil in a large skillet over medium-high heat. When it is very hot, add the curry powder. Cook, stirring, for 2 minutes. Add the onion, scallion, garlic, sweet pepper, Scotch bonnet pepper and black pepper. Cook, stirring constantly, for 3 minutes. Add the tomato sauce or paste and cook 3 minutes more. Add the water and blend well.

■ Add the okra and shrimp. Reduce the heat to medium, cover and cook until the shrimp are just cooked through, about 5 minutes. It is best served hot, straight out of the pan.

NOTE—The shrimp heads, tails and shells can be left on for better flavor and a more rustic dining experience.

COCONUT SHRIMP

MAKES 6 TO 8 SERVINGS

The nutty toasted coconut complements the shrimp flavor perfectly. This makes a great appetizer served with the spicy dipping sauce.

FOR THE SAUCE
2 teaspoons Scotch bonnet pepper (any color), seeded and minced
Juice of 1 lime
1 tablespoon honey
1 tablespoon dark rum
½ teaspoon salt
1 tablespoon vegetable oil

FOR THE SHRIMP
1 pound medium shrimp, peeled and deveined
2 egg whites
½ teaspoon Worcestershire sauce
¼ teaspoon salt
1 cup shredded, unsweetened coconut
½ cup vegetable oil

■ For the sauce, combine the Scotch bonnet pepper, lime juice, honey, rum, salt and oil in a serving bowl. Set aside.

■ Rinse the shrimp in cold water and pat dry with paper towels. In a small bowl, beat together the egg whites, Worcestershire sauce and salt. Spread the coconut out on a plate. Coat each shrimp with the egg white mixture and roll in the coconut.

■ Heat ¼ cup of the oil in a large skillet over high heat until it is very hot. Add half of the shrimp to the oil in a single layer. Fry until golden brown, for 1½ minutes. Turn each one over and cook 2 minutes more. Remove to drain on paper towels. Using the remaining ¼ cup of oil, repeat the process until all of the shrimp is cooked. Serve the shrimp immediately with the dipping sauce.

MANGO CHUTNEY

MAKES 3 CUPS

This chutney is a natural accompaniment for any of the curry dishes.

4 mangoes, peeled, pitted and chopped
   (4 cups)
3 tablespoons grated fresh ginger
1 onion, chopped
1 clove garlic, minced
½ sweet red pepper, seeded and chopped
   (about 1 cup)
½ cup raisins
⅓ cup sugar
2 teaspoons salt
½ cup white vinegar
⅓ cup water

■ Mix all of the ingredients together in a noncorrosive saucepan. Bring to a boil over high heat, then reduce the heat to low and simmer for 1 hour and 15 minutes. Remove from the heat and allow the chutney to cool. Store in glass jars in the refrigerator up to 6 months.

PAWPAW PEPPER SAUCE

MAKES 2 1/2 CUPS

Many people keep their own homemade hot sauce on hand or at least a favorite commercial sauce. Jamaicans use it like ketchup. This sauce is spicy, yet flavorful, and simple to prepare. The pawpaw sweetens and texturizes the vegetable base and provides a gentle palette for the robust Scotch bonnet peppers.

3 carrots, peeled
1 chocho (chayote), peeled and pitted, or 1 medium cucumber, peeled and seeded
6 Scotch bonnet peppers (any color)
1 small or ½ large pawpaw (papaya), peeled and seeded
2 teaspoons salt
1 teaspoon brown sugar
⅓ cup white vinegar
¾ cup water

■ Place the carrots and chocho in a food processor or blender. Blend until pulverized. Remove the stems from the Scotch bonnet peppers and add the peppers to the carrots and chocho. Blend until the mixture is an even consistency. Add the pawpaw, continuing to blend until you have a uniform texture.

■ Place the mixture into a noncorrosive saucepan. Add the salt, brown sugar, vinegar and water. Bring it to a boil over high heat, then reduce the heat to low and cover. Simmer it for 30 minutes. Remove from the heat and let cool completely. Place in small bottles or jars. Keep it refrigerated.

JERK SAUCE

MAKES 1 QUART

The basis for righteous jerk barbecue is great sauce. Sauce varies among the experts, recipes are coveted and shrouded in secrecy, yet basic flavors dominate. Chief among them, the pimento tree has given jerking its young green branches for patas (grill stands) and its berries (allspice) for seasoning. In this recipe, jerk sauce is pared down to its bare essentials. Many Jamaicans have different recipes, which include cinnamon or ginger or nutmeg or you name it. Build your own sauce to taste; this is not a science, it's an art! How much fiery Scotch bonnet pepper to use is a controversy that rages among family and friends. Tested on both wimps and fire-eaters, this sauce challenges the former and leaves macho mouths clamoring, "Make it spicier next time." For them, just splash in some hot pepper and line up the cold Red Stripes.

5 bunches whole scallions, finely chopped
3 large cloves garlic, minced
3 Scotch bonnet peppers (any color), seeded and minced
2 large sprigs fresh thyme or 2 tablespoons dried
¼ cup ground allspice (dry pimento berries)
2 tablespoons freshly ground black pepper
1½ tablespoons salt
1 cup water

■ In a large bowl, combine all the ingredients except the water. Mix well and add water to form a loose paste.

NOTE—Sources for specialty wood chips often carry dried pimento leaves, which add additional flavor to the fire at barbecue time.

PINEAPPLE JAM

MAKES 2 CUPS

It's hard to imagine a more luscious combination than pineapple jam spread over a slice of toasted Coconut Bread (page 109). This jam also makes a good foundation for sweet-and-sour sauce or a glaze for roasted meats.

**1 pineapple
1 cup water
2 cups sugar
Juice of 2 limes**

■ Peel and grate the pineapple, reserving the peel for Pineappleade (page 117).

■ Grate the flesh—you should end up with about 2 cups. Put the pineapple and water in a small saucepan and cook over medium-low heat until the pineapple is soft, about 35 minutes.

■ Add the sugar and lime juice and stir to combine. Cook until the mixture has thickened, 45 to 60 minutes. Spoon the jam into a 16-ounce jar and seal. Keep it in the refrigerator up to 6 months.

DESSERTS
AND
DRINKS

COCONUT CREAM PIE

MAKES 8 SERVINGS

Practically everyone loves coconut cream pie. Made with a real custard filling and meringue on top, this is a sure dessert favorite. If you can't use fresh coconut, shredded, unsweetened coconut in a package will do fine, as will a commercially prepared pie shell.

FOR THE PASTRY
1¼ cups all-purpose flour
⅛ teaspoon salt
¼ cup margarine or lard, chilled (½ stick)
2 tablespoons butter, chilled
3 tablespoons ice-cold water

FOR THE FILLING
½ cup all-purpose flour
½ cup plus 5 tablespoons sugar
⅛ teaspoon salt
2 cups milk
3 eggs, separated
2 tablespoons butter
1 teaspoon vanilla
1 cup plus 1 tablespoon shredded, unsweetened coconut

■ To prepare the pastry, in a large bowl, combine the flour and salt. Cut the margarine and butter into small pieces and add it to the bowl. Working quickly using a knife or pastry blender, cut the flour and fat together until the mixture resembles a coarse meal. Sprinkle the water over the surface, mixing it quickly just until the dough forms a smooth ball. Separate the dough into 2 pieces and flatten them into disks. Refrigerate them until needed.

■ For the filling, in a bowl that will fit over a pan of boiling water (or a double boiler), combine the flour, ½ cup of sugar and salt. Heat the milk in a heavy saucepan over medium-high until small bubbles appear at the edge of the milk. Using a whisk to stir, pour the scalded milk into the flour mixture and cook over medium heat until it thickens, 2 to 3 minutes.

■ In a large bowl, whisk together the egg yolks and add 1 tablespoon of the hot custard mixture. Blend well. Whisk the egg yolk mixture into the custard (still on the stove top). Blend in the butter and vanilla. Cook 2 minutes more. Remove the bowl from the heat and let cool, stirring it a couple of times. Fold in 1 cup of the coconut.

■ Preheat the oven to 400°F. Roll one piece of the chilled dough on a floured surface to a thickness of ⅛ inch and fit it into a 9-inch pie pan (refrigerate the other piece of pastry for another occasion). Fold over the edges of the pastry and pinch it all around. Line the pastry with wax paper or foil and weigh it down with dried beans or pebbles. Blind bake the crust for 13 minutes.

■ Reduce the oven temperature to 350°F. Remove the paper and weights.

■ In a large bowl, whip the egg whites until stiff. Add the remaining 5 tablespoons of sugar and continue to whip for 2 minutes until it is glossy and peaks stand up when the beater is removed (stiff peaks are formed).

■ Spoon the custard filling into the cooked pie crust. Smooth it out evenly. Spread the meringue over the filling. Bake for 10 to 15 minutes, or until the meringue is lightly browned. Sprinkle remaining tablespoon of coconut on top before serving.

VARIATION—To make Banana Cream Pie, omit the coconut from the custard and place 2 sliced ripe bananas on top of the custard.

NOTE—The meringue will cut more easily if the knife is dipped in warm water before making each slice.

BANANA CAKE

MAKES 8 SERVINGS

A crispy brown sugar and butter topping elevates this moist and delicious cake above most ordinary recipes.

2 cups all-purpose flour
1½ teaspoons baking powder
1 teaspoon baking soda
¾ teaspoon salt
¾ cup sugar
½ cup butter, melted (1 stick)
½ cup buttermilk, yogurt or milk
2 eggs
1 teaspoon vanilla
2 ripe bananas, mashed (about 1 cup)

FOR THE TOPPING
¼ cup all-purpose flour
¼ cup dark brown sugar
¼ cup butter (½ stick)

■ Preheat the oven to 300°F. In a large bowl, combine the flour, baking powder, baking soda, salt and sugar. Blend in the melted butter, mixing together until moist. Add ¼ cup of the buttermilk and combine.

■ In a separate bowl, combine the other ¼ cup of buttermilk with the eggs and blend into the flour mixture. Add the vanilla and mashed bananas. Beat for 1 minute. Place the batter in a greased 9x13x2-inch pan.

■ To make the topping, squeeze the flour, brown sugar and butter together with your hands. Crumble the topping evenly over the batter. Bake for 35 to 40 minutes. When the cake is done, an inserted toothpick or fork should come out clean from the center.

NOTE—Buttermilk is the preferred liquid for this recipe, but it is equally successful with a combination of milk and plain yogurt or with milk alone.

BAKED BANANAS

Nothing melts in the mouth like baked bananas. Served with any kind of cream topping, it is a simple, unsurpassed dessert. Adjust the ingredients and flavors to your personal taste.

2 bananas
Juice of 1 lime
1 tablespoon dark rum
¼ teaspoon ground cinnamon
⅛ teaspoon ground nutmeg
1 tablespoon dark brown sugar
1 tablespoon butter (optional)

■ Preheat the oven to 400°F. Peel the bananas and slice in half lengthwise. Lay the pieces into a buttered 9x13x2-inch ovenproof dish. Pour the lime juice and rum evenly over the bananas. Sprinkle on the cinnamon, nutmeg and brown sugar. Dot on the butter, if using, and bake for 10 to 15 minutes. Serve hot, topped with a tablespoon of fresh cream or ice cream.

BREAD PUDDING WITH RUM SAUCE

MAKES 8 SERVINGS

This dessert is a great way to use up stale bread, but it is so good you might just buy fresh bread especially to make it. Serve with a scoop of mango ice cream.

FOR THE PUDDING
¼ cup raisins
2 tablespoons dark rum
12 slices white bread, preferably slightly stale (about ½ pound)
1 cup milk
1 cup coconut milk
2 eggs
¾ cup sugar
½ teaspoon vanilla
½ teaspoon cinnamon
¼ teaspoon ground nutmeg

FOR THE SAUCE
¾ cup dark brown sugar
⅓ cup water
½ cup butter (1 stick)
¼ cup dark rum

▓ Preheat the oven to 350°F. Grease a 9x13x2-inch ovenproof baking dish. In a small bowl, combine the raisins and rum and set aside.

▓ Remove the crusts from the bread. In a blender or food processor, blend the crusts into bread crumbs. Set aside 3 tablespoons and reserve the rest for another use. Cube the bread and put the pieces into a large bowl. Pour the milk and coconut milk over the bread. Set aside to saturate completely.

▓ In a separate bowl, beat together the eggs, sugar, vanilla, cinnamon and nutmeg. Pour it over the bread along with the raisins and rum. Stir the mixture until well blended. Pour it into the baking dish and sprinkle the 3 tablespoons of bread crumbs over the top. Bake for 40 minutes.

▓ Meanwhile, prepare the sauce. In a small saucepan, combine the brown sugar, water, butter and rum. Bring to a boil over medium-high heat and boil gently until thickened, about 10 minutes. Pour a little over each portion when serving.

PINEAPPLE UPSIDE-DOWN CAKE

MAKES 8 SERVINGS

This old-fashioned cake cooked in a cast-iron skillet remains one of my favorite desserts. Canned pineapple will work but doesn't come close to the heavenly flavor of a fresh, ripe "pine" combined with butter and brown sugar.

1⅓ cups all-purpose flour
¾ cup sugar
2 teaspoons baking powder
½ teaspoon salt
¼ cup vegetable oil
¾ cup milk
1 teaspoon vanilla
1 egg
Grated rind from 1 lime
1 tablespoon fresh lime juice
¼ cup butter (½ stick)
½ cup dark brown sugar
1 fresh, ripe pineapple, sliced, or one
   20-ounce can pineapple slices
15 pecans

▪ Preheat the oven to 350°F. In a mixing bowl, sift together the flour, sugar, baking powder and salt. Add the oil and milk to the bowl and beat for 1 minute. Add the vanilla, egg, lime rind and lime juice, blending just until well combined.

▪ In a cast-iron skillet over medium heat, melt the butter. Remove from the heat and sprinkle the brown sugar around the skillet. Arrange the pineapple slices and pecans on top. Pour the batter evenly over the top and bake for 45 minutes.

▪ Remove from the oven and cool the cake in the pan for 5 minutes. Turn the cake out onto a circular platter.

JACKASS CORN

MAKES 12 TO 15 BISCUITS

This crunchy snack will keep for a long time. Yet another clever Jamaican expression, its name reputedly comes from the sounds made during eating, which resemble a jackass chewing on his corn.

1 cup all-purpose flour
¼ teaspoon baking soda
1 cup sugar
½ teaspoon ground nutmeg
¼ teaspoon salt
1 cup shredded, unsweetened coconut
3 tablespoons water

■ Preheat the oven to 375°F. In a medium-size bowl, combine the flour, baking soda, sugar, nutmeg and salt. Stir in the coconut. Add the water and mix, forming a very stiff dough that will not crumble.

■ Roll out the dough on a floured board to ⅛-inch thickness. Cut the dough into small rectangles. Place the pieces onto a greased cookie sheet and prick each one with a fork. Bake for 8 to 9 minutes, or until brown. Remove from the oven and transfer to a plate to cool.

COCONUT BREAD

MAKES 1 LOAF OR 8 SLICES

Serve this sliced and toasted with butter and Pineapple Jam (page 95) for a special breakfast treat.

1½ cups all-purpose flour
2 teaspoons baking powder
½ teaspoon salt
½ cup sugar
1 egg, lightly beaten
1 teaspoon vanilla
½ cup milk
½ cup grated dried coconut

■ Preheat the oven to 350°F. In a bowl, combine the flour, baking powder, salt and sugar. Add the egg and vanilla and mix. Add the milk and coconut and mix until well combined. Put in a small greased loaf pan. Bake for 1 hour, or until the bread is springy to the touch. Remove from the oven and let cool in the pan for 5 minutes. Turn the bread out onto a wire rack to cool before slicing.

VARIATION—For a more concentrated flavor, use coconut milk in place of regular milk.

LIMEADE

With the abundance of limes in Jamaica, limeade is a common drink. Even the commonly bottled unsweetened lime juice is excellent paired with bottled sugar syrup for a quick limeade. As an alternative to sugar, try honey, which, combined with lime juice, is an excellent aid for the respiratory system.

5 to 7 medium-size limes
5 cups water (40 ounces)
½ cup honey or sugar

■ For the maximum juice, roll the limes over the counter back and forth with the palm of your hand. Cut the limes in half and juice them by hand or with a juicer (reserving the rinds). You should have about ½ cup (4 ounces) of juice. Place the rinds and the juice in a large pitcher.

■ Place 1 cup of the water in a saucepan over high heat. When it boils, add the honey or sugar and mix until it dissolves. Pour this mixture into the pitcher along with the remaining water. Blend well and taste for sweetness. Refrigerate it for 1 hour. Remove the rinds and discard.

VARIATION—For super flavor and enriched medicinal value, add slices of fresh ginger to the pitcher along with the rinds.

LIME SQUASH

MAKES TWO 8-OUNCE DRINKS

4 small or 2 medium-size limes
3 tablespoons honey
1¼ cups carbonated water
   (mineral water, club soda, etc.)
   (10 ounces)

This refreshing, carbonated drink is a great, healthy alternative to soda.

■ For the maximum juice, roll the limes over the counter back and forth with the palm of your hand. Cut the limes in half and juice them by hand or with a juicer. You should have ½ cup (4 ounces) of juice. Put the juice and honey into a bowl and mix well with a wire whisk or fork. Pour the mixture into a pitcher. Add the carbonated water and stir until all of the ingredients are well combined. Taste and adjust it for the desired sweetness. Serve it over ice.

VARIATION—Lemons can be used in place of limes.

RUM PUNCH

MAKES FIVE 8-OUNCE SERVINGS

Several years ago, we arrived at this simple formula after tasting and testing many versions for a Jamaican restaurant. It's a rough job, but someone has to do it. Try creating your own by mixing a few different fruit juices with your favorite rum.

2¼ cups unsweetened pineapple juice (18 ounces)
2 cups guava juice (16 ounces)
Juice of 3 medium-size limes
½ cup dark Jamaican rum (4 ounces) (Appleton)

■ Mix all of the ingredients well and chill. Serve over ice, dressed with tropical fruit. Splash on an extra hit of rum before serving if desired.

CLASSIC JAMAICAN RUM PUNCH

YIELD: YOU DECIDE.

1 part sour
2 parts sweet
3 parts strong
4 parts weak

This classic formula turns up in all of the written discussions of Jamaican drinks. It's the proportions that matter, so interpret it your own way. I will say that sour equals lime juice and strong equals rum. Sweet could be sugar water or a concentrated juice and weak is water or a light juice.

■ Mix well and serve over crushed ice.

GINGER BEER

Jamaicans love their ginger beer. Without a doubt, the natural abundance of ginger on the island and its superior quality accounts for its popularity. These days ginger beer is widely available and rarely made at home. But homemade ginger beer is easy to make and just requires yeast for fermentation. It is well worth the effort.

¼ cup grated fresh ginger
¾ cup sugar
4 cups water (32 ounces)
Juice of ½ lime
½ packet dry yeast

■ Combine all of the ingredients in a large pitcher. Stir and allow to sit at room temperature for 24 hours. Strain and refrigerate. Serve chilled.

SORREL DRINK

MAKES TWELVE 8-OUNCE SERVINGS

No discussion of Jamaican beverages would be complete without mention of sorrel, which is a festive offering at Christmas and New Year's. This radiant red-flowering plant, a member of the hibiscus family, makes a fragrant drink with a zesty taste. It is also served with white rum as an unusual cocktail. Dried sorrel can be found packaged at some specialty stores. Use 3 to 4 cups if using dried leaves.

6 cups sorrel sepals, removed from the stalk
1-inch piece fresh ginger, sliced
Three 2-inch pieces orange peel
5 allspice berries (dry pimento berries), crushed
3 whole cloves, crushed
12 cups boiling water (96 ounces)
1½ cups sugar
Juice of 1 lime

■ Place the sorrel, ginger, orange peel, allspice and cloves in a large heatproof pitcher or bowl. Pour in 10 cups of the boiling water and stir. Cover and leave it to steep for 24 hours. Strain out the liquid through a sieve. Boil the remaining 2 cups of water and blend it with the sugar until dissolved. Add the sugar water to the strained liquid along with the lime juice. Stir to blend it completely. Sweeten it further if desired. Serve over crushed ice.

PINEAPPLEADE

This frugal drink utilizes the peel of the pineapple. It's a sin not to make this drink every time you use the flesh of a fresh pineapple. You'll never carelessly discard the peel again once you've tasted this thirst-quenching treat.

4 cups water (32 ounces)
1 pineapple
½ cup sugar
2 whole cloves
½-inch piece grated fresh ginger (1 teaspoon)

■ Bring the water to a boil in a saucepan over high heat. Wash and peel the pineapple and place the peel, sugar, cloves and ginger into a large heatproof pitcher. (Save the rest of the pineapple for another use.) Pour the boiling water into the pitcher and stir. Let it sit at room temperature for 24 hours. Strain and serve chilled or over ice.

BANANA DAIQUIRI

MAKES TWO 8-OUNCE SERVINGS

This frozen drink is a happy hour favorite at north coast resorts. It tastes like dessert and slides down so smoothly, but beware of the creeping rum sensation.

¾ cup rum (6 ounces)
1½ ripe bananas, peeled
Juice of 1 lime
1 strip lime rind
3½ tablespoons sugar
10 ice cubes

■ Combine all of the ingredients in a blender jar and blend on high speed until the texture is smooth. Serve in glasses with a lime wedge and an extra splash of rum.

PAWPAW DRINK

Pawpaw is the fruit that many folks know as papaya. It is an excellent digestive aid. Serve this along with any fiercely spiced meat dish.

1 ripe pawpaw (papaya)
2 oranges
1 lime
1 slice fresh ginger
3 tablespoons honey
4 ice cubes

■ Slice the pawpaw in half. Scoop out the seeds and discard. Scoop the flesh into a blender jar. Cut the oranges and lime in half and juice by hand or with a juicer. Add the juice to the blender jar. Add the ginger, honey and ice cubes and blend until it is well combined with a smooth, slushy texture.

INDEX